"With exquisite un[...] each family's needs, Kathleen Finley has produced a much needed resource for parents seeking to enrich the spiritual life of their children. She beautifully marries her training as a theologian and her experience as a mother to provide us with a prayer guide that cannot but be a grace-full experience for all who use it, parents and children alike."

Clayton C. Barbeau, F.F.C.T.
Author, *The Father of the Family*

"Kathleen Finley has authored a book that should be tops on the list for parents who want to pray with their children. *Dear God: Prayers for Families with Children* brings God into the everyday existence of a family. The prayers in it deal with subjects that are part of a child's world and use language that is meaningful to a child. They could be a stepping stone for families wanting to compose their own spontaneous prayers."

Kay and Gary Aitchison
Executive Directors
Christian Family Movement

"I'm pleased to recommend *Dear God* to families with young children hoping to grow in household faith. They will find many simple and creative ways to use this book, and it will fit right into the hustle and bustle of their household life. The book is also a great gift idea. I know several families I want to give it to."

Leif Kehrwald
Independent Family Ministry Consultant
Author, *Family Spirituality: The Raw Ingredients of Faith*

"Kathy Finley's *Dear God* is a treasury of down-home prayers that will help parents 'prime the pump' of prayer in their families. These simple, everyday prayers will inspire moms, dads, and kids to love the Lord more. Best of all, they will teach children how to speak with God in their own words about the things that concern them most."

Bert Ghezzi
Author, *Guiltless Catholic Parenting*
and *Keeping Your Kids Catholic*

"*Dear God* is a splendid gift for today's families with children. This book of simple, informal prayers is a wonderful resource to help families make ordinary, sometimes mundane, moments holy. Kathleen Finley's prayers capture everyday family situations and see in them God's constant presence and care: the death of a pet, birthdays, a new house, vacations, the first and last day of school, illnesses, winning and losing, finding a treasure, losing a tooth, as well as prayers for religious and natural occasions and seasons.

"The variety of prayers is a wonderful start for young families. I can see this book helping families confidently and comfortably devise their own prayers for other personal, ordinary times. In addition, *Dear God* is more than a book of prayers. It is a discussion starter and a celebration of family life—warts and all. Thanks, Kathleen, for helping families and children talk easily and comfortably to and about God."

Sandra DeGidio, O.S.M.
Author, *Enriching Faith through Family Celebrations,*
Sacraments Alive, and *Prayer Services for the Elderly*

Dear God

PRAYERS FOR FAMILIES WITH CHILDREN

KATHLEEN FINLEY

Illustrations by Kevin Finley

TWENTY-THIRD PUBLICATIONS

Mystic, CT 06355

Second printing 1995

Twenty-Third Publications
185 Willow Street
P.O. Box 180
Mystic, CT 06355
(203) 536-2611
800-321-0411

ISBN 0-89622-673-5
Library of Congress Catalog Card Number 95-61647
Printed in the U.S.A.

Dedication

This book is for my husband, Mitch
and my sons Sean, Patrick, and Kevin
with whom I have shared prayer
during many special times,
and who tolerate
my deep love of celebration.

Table of Contents

Special Occasion Prayers

Introduction

What happens in your home is very important and very holy. Did that statement get your attention? If you're like most parents, maybe you'd be willing to admit the "important" part; "holy" is harder to agree with. Did you say to yourself, "But you haven't been to my house"?

This book is based on a very simple yet important idea: Your home, any home, is where the Good News is first lived, communicated, felt, and celebrated. It is at home that we first find (or don't find), a sense of God—not just words about God, but a real sense of being loved just as we are. This is the Good News that we share with others in our parishes, neighborhoods, workplaces, and elsewhere.

Further, family prayer and celebration are not about *making* family life holy or bringing God into your home, but about realizing the holiness that is *already* there. (See the Suggested Resources at the end of the book for more about this idea.) The challenge for us as parents is to look again—literally to *re-spect*—what is right before our eyes in our own homes.

Many who grew up in families that embraced Catholic or other Christian traditions were surrounded by practices and objects that helped nurture their spirituality and remind them of their faith, from novenas to holy cards to rosaries to special clothes for First Communion. (When my husband and I ask participants in our workshops to generate a list of the Catholic "artifacts" they remember from childhood, the list seems to get longer the older the group is or the farther East we go!)

Many once-common religious practices fell out of favor after the Second Vatican Council. Though these changes were made in keeping with the spirit of the Council, it left a gap in religious expression for many people. Parents of today may well ask themselves: What is the faith we have to offer our children, and how can we create an environment that helps make them people of faith?

In the early days of Christianity, the family was seen as the domestic church, the basic community of faith on which the larger church was founded. As we rediscover the holiness of our families and homes, our spirituality can begin to focus on God's presence in our daily lives. This means less emphasis on church as the Holy—notice the capital "H"—place where God dwells, and more emphasis on the holy—small "h"—places and times in our midst.

In the last twenty years or so, we have witnessed a considerable change in the way families are structured. The majority of small children either grow up in households where both parents work outside the home, or they live in single-parent households. This book attempts to take the diversity of families today into account. If a particular prayer does not fit your situation, however, modify it for your needs.

Prayer should become a habit, one which we can help teach

our children much as we teach them habits of good hygiene and manners. Of course, this does not guarantee that they will continue these habits once they have left our homes, but we will have planted the seeds for lifelong prayer.

Begin early to pray with your children. I am convinced that the most "teachable moment" for both family and individual prayer is when children are between the ages of three and twelve. It is difficult in the teen or preteen years to initiate family customs that were not begun earlier; just ask a parent of adolescents.

The prayers found in this book reflect what our three sons have taught me and what we have taught each other about prayer over the years. Our prayer experiences have ranged from a parade with palms and rhythm instruments on Palm Sunday, to a simple Stations of the Cross (complete with a kitchen hand towel for Veronica's veil, a plastic hammer to nail Jesus to the cross, and a large pillow for Jesus' tomb), to a blessing of the riding toys in the front yard.

If we listen, our children can teach us much about God. In the book *Chicken Soup for the Soul*, Dan Millman tells of four-year-old Sacha asking to be left alone with her newborn baby brother. Through a crack in the door her parents could see her go over quietly and put her face close to his, saying, "Baby, tell me what God feels like. I'm starting to forget."

Family Prayer and Celebration
Many of us did not grow up with the ability to speak comfortably about our relationship with God. Faith was often a strong-

ly personal area of our lives that one lived out but didn't mention in conversation.

The prayers in *Dear God* are written in an informal, spontaneous style. They are like having a conversation with God. Many families find this a natural way to help their children develop an open and loving relationship with God; for parents, too, spontaneous prayer can be both exciting and liberating.

Many books on family prayer seem too formal for most families, with overly "liturgical" elements like a fixed response to a psalm or a litany. Family prayer, in my experience, happens within the events and occurrences of ordinary—and extraordinary—life, and is usually rather informal.

This book addresses God in a personal and loving way, but without limiting images of God to male (or female) ones. Perhaps our children will figure out a way to be inclusive in our images of God and yet preserve the best in the Judeo-Christian tradition.

Traditional prayer also holds a very important place in the life of the family. There are a number of resources available to help teach these prayers. It's also important to introduce Scripture to children. You can do this through Bible stories as well as with phrases from Scripture that a young child can remember and savor, such as, "Let the little children come to me," or "I am the light of the world."

Prayer often needs a focal point, especially when young children are involved. Think about your home: What would you identify as the holiest place there? In many families, it's the family table, where they are most often all together (although the family meal seems to be an endangered species in our over-busy society).

In our family, a candle on the table helps us focus on prayer, reminding us that Jesus is the light of the world and that he's present where two or more are gathered in his name. We also join hands as we pray, to remind ourselves of our oneness. (Keep in mind the natural chaos of family life; many a night someone at our table has announced that "no way" would he hold his brother's hand!)

When introducing family prayer, it's wise to begin simply, perhaps with a prayer at dinner or a blessing at bedtime. If it is comfortable for you and your child, trace a cross on your child's forehead before bed or when he or she leaves the house. Singing familiar songs at prayer times and family celebrations can also be powerful.

Look at your family's rhythms and needs. For example, I know a family with grade-school children who would gather to study the Bible for half an hour before everyone left for the day. It was a great idea, but it would never have worked at our house: We're lucky if everyone gets out the door on time!

Another family says grace after their meal, so they can eat their food while it's hot and concentrate better on prayer when they're not as hungry. Just as our individual spiritualities are different, so are our family spiritualities; your family's will look unique because your family is unique.

Involve as many members of your family in planning prayer as possible. Those with musical or artistic talent can contribute songs and pictures: Even young children can help read and lead prayers. Don't be afraid to evaluate how a prayer time went; several times when our children were small I overestimated their attention span with prayers that went too long.

How to Use This Book

Please consider this a book of suggestions, to be used much as a confident cook would use a cookbook ("They say a half teaspoon of thyme; I think I'll try a whole teaspoon, since I like thyme.") Make this book your own to fit your family and their needs.

Use *Dear God* as a resource for the busy times, when we are lucky to get the birthday or Thanksgiving meal on the table, let alone give some thought to the prayer. At such times in my house, I would most often grab a book that is sadly now out of print, *Prayer After Nine Rainy Days and Other Family Prayers*, by Pat Corrick Hinton, to which this book owes its inspiration.

Family prayer happens within family life. Take a look at how this book is structured, with prayers for every day, for the seasons of the year as well as the liturgical season, and for special occasions. Read through the book ahead of time to help you recognize similar occasions as they occur in your family's life and to be ready to use these prayers at those times.

May the use of this book draw you closer to God and to a deeper realization of God's presence in the midst of your family—a messy and holy place.

DAILY
PRAYERS

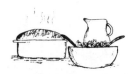

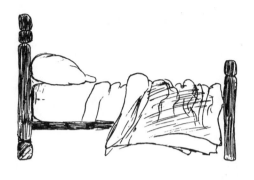

Waking Up

Good morning, God.
Thank you for the day
    that is just beginning.
It's like a shiny, new present
    that hasn't been opened yet.
As I open it today,
    help me to watch for
    all the special ways
    you show me that you love me;
    all the invisible gift tags that say,
    "To you, with great love, God."
Thanks again for today.
Help me to show my thanks
    by loving others as you love me
    and by using with great care
    the world you've given us. Amen.

Before Leaving for the Day or on a Trip

Dear God,
> please bless each of us
> as we leave today
> to go to (name destination).

Please help us to remember
> that you go with us wherever we are.

Help us to bring you to others
> and see you in the people
> we are with today.

And please keep us safe
> until we are back together again.

Amen.

Parent's Note: This prayer may be said as family members go off to school or work, or can be used as a family member leaves for a trip. Bless the departing person by making a sign of the cross on their forehead as you say this prayer, if this gesture is comfortable for you and your family.

Meal Prayers

Dear God,
    thank you
    for this day,
    for each other,
    for the food
    before us,

And for all who helped to grow
    and cook this food.
We remember our world
    and all those who
    need our prayers today.
Let this meal
    nourish our hearts and souls
    as well as our bodies. Amen.

Dear God,
    please bless this food and us
    who gather around it.
And thank you for all
    your gifts to us.
Amen.

Parent's Note: These are two forms of grace before meals. As an alternative to spoken grace, you might consider a moment of silence, followed by an "Amen" ; or, have everyone name one thing they are grateful for; or, sing a short song, such as an "Amen" or "The Lord is good to me...."

Before Reading Together

Dear God,
Thank you for this time together
    to cuddle up and read.
Thank you for books
    that help us travel to other places and times.
Thank you for those who helped create this book
    and for our own imaginations.
And thank you for books
    that help us think
    about different people and ways of life.
Please help us remember
    that the best story of all
        is the one about
          how much you love us.
                Amen.

Prayer for Bath or Shower

Dear God,
    thanks for my body
    and for the water to wash it with.
When I'm all clean I feel
    almost like a little baby again.
Thanks for soap and shampoo
    and washcloths and towels
    and the chance to feel new again.
Amen.

Bedtime Blessing

May God watch over you while you sleep
and give you good dreams.
May you have a peaceful night. Amen.

Parent's Note: The nightly blessing is a powerful ritual, one that should be taught early in a child's life. The above (or similar words) may be said while tracing a cross on the child's forehead. Some parents may want to mention the child's guardian angel, which is a vivid way to image God's help and care for each of us.

SEASONAL
PRAYERS

First Day of School

Loving God,
    school is about to start for the year.
We're excited
    and a little bit scared
    about what this year might hold.
Please help us to remember
    that you are there with us
    at new beginnings:
To get used to new rooms,
    and new teachers,
    and new skills
    to be learned.
Help us
    on the good days,
    but especially
    on the bad days.
Help us to do
    our very best,
    and to keep
    learning about you
    and the world
    you gave us.
Amen.

On a Fall Day

God of all the colors of the rainbow,
    thank you
    for this amazing fall day
    when the leaves are bright with hues.
You made these leaves
    for us to enjoy,
    to give us shade in summer
    and to see life in a whole new way
    as they begin to fall and die.
Their dying now will make room
    for new life next spring;

Just as when we die
    to the selfishness inside
    we make room for your new life in us.
You made each one of us
    as different and unique
    as each of these leaves,
    each very special to you.
Help us to see your love
    in many ways all around us,
    and to enjoy this
    colorful time of year.
Amen.

21

Halloween

Loving God,
    this is a scary time of year,
    with our thoughts full
    of ghosts and goblins and witches.
It's also a fun time of year
    with costumes and masks and candy.
Help us to remember that
    you are always watching us
    and caring for us;
Your love has lots of treats
    and no tricks.
Please bless all who have died
    and whose feasts
    we celebrate
    over the next few days.
Keep us safe
    as we take part
    in this spooky
    fun holiday.
Amen.

Parent's Note: The church celebrates All Saints' Day on November 1, and All Souls' Day on November 2. You may want to talk about these feast days with your family; see Suggested Resources for where to find more information on these holy days.

Thanksgiving

Dear God,
    where do we begin to say thanks?
You have given us all that we have:
You have given us one another,
    the ability to run, to think, to love
    and to say "thank you" to you.
As we gather today
    with special foods,
Help us to remember
    that every day
    is a day
    to give you thanks.
Please bless your children
    who do not have
    as much as we do,
And help us understand
    how to share
    what we have with them.
Thank you again
    for all your gifts.
Amen.

Parent's Note: Use this prayer for grace at
your Thanksgiving Day meal. After the prayer has been said, each
person at the table may want to mention one thing for which they
are especially thankful.

On the First Snow

It's snowing, Lord;
    there's a white miracle outside!
The snow is covering everything
    the grass, the trees,
    the buildings, and streets.
It reminds us of your love:
Like this magical snow
    your love covers and surrounds us
    and everything around us,
    even when we don't think about it
    or can't see it.
Thank you
    for the white wonder of snow,
    and for the chance
    to have fun in it.
Thank you
    for the cold,
    and the quiet
    beauty it brings
And thank you
    for your love.
Amen.

St. Nicholas Day

Dear God,
     thank you for the gift of St. Nicholas,
     a most wonderful man.
He loved people, especially children,
     and he was very generous.
Help us to remember
     to be loving and generous
     especially as we prepare
     for the feast of
     Christmas.
Help us to
     decorate our hearts
     as well as our homes
     at this special time of year.
Amen.

Parent's Note: The feast of St. Nicholas, the historical figure on whom Santa Claus is based, is celebrated on December 6th in many parts of the world. It is a time for children to put out their shoes or stockings the evening before, only to find a treat there in the morning.

Practicing this tradition in your home can help ease the long wait until Christmas. The feast of St. Nicholas is also a good time to think about ways we can help those in need, for example, with a visit to a lonely neighbor, or with a contribution to the local food bank or "Toys for Tots" drive.

First Week of Advent
(For use with an Advent wreath)

Dear God,
    Christmas is only a month away.
Help us to prepare for Jesus' birth
    during this Advent season.
Our first candle
    reminds us of the light of hope
    that the prophets had
    as they looked toward a Messiah
    who would bring peace and love to the world.
Dear God, our world is in darkness.
We need the light of peace and love
    to shine in our world.
Help us to prepare our lives and our homes
    to receive Jesus, who said,
    "I am the light of the world." Amen.

(Sing "O Come, O Come Emmanuel.")

Second Week of Advent

Dear God,
  our second candle reminds us
  of the dark night when Joseph and Mary
  found light and warmth in the stable.
Help us to have room in our hearts and in our home
  for other persons who need us.
We thank you for friends and strangers
  who have received us
  when we are lonely, or afraid, or tired.
Thank you for those who listen to us,
  hug us, and care for us when we're sick or sad.
Please help us to love others in those same ways.
Amen.

(Sing "Away in a Manger.")

Parent's Note: The children might want to send a note and/or a drawing to someone who has shown them love or kindness.

Third Week of Advent

Dear God,
  our third candle reminds us
  of the love and joy
  which surrounded the shepherds
  at the news of Jesus' birth.
Thank you for your gift
  of Jesus
  to the whole world.
As the shepherds
  found Jesus in a
  manger,
  may we find
  Jesus
  in the love
  and joy
  that we share together.
Help us to love one another.
Help us to do our share
  to bring happiness, goodness,
  and peace to the world.
Amen.

(Sing "The First Noel.")

28

Fourth Week of Advent

Dear God,
    our fourth candle reminds us
    of the star which guided the Magi
    to the stable where Jesus lay.
Thank you for sharing Jesus with all the world.
Please help us to care about
    and make friends with
    those who may be different from us.
Help us, too, to remember
    that the gifts we share
    with each other at Christmas
    are reminders of the gift that Jesus is to us.
Amen.

(Sing "We Three Kings of Orient Are.")

Christmas

It's finally here!
Dear God,
    the day we've been waiting
    and preparing for is here,
    the birthday of your son, Jesus.
Today we rejoice
    with the animals
    and the shepherds,
    with the angels
    and the stars;

With the Magi
and all the world.
For you gave us
the greatest gift of all:
You gave us Jesus.
He showed us the way to live
and the way to love;
He is your show-and-tell.
Help us remember
as we open our gifts
and eat special foods
that it's Jesus
we celebrate today.
Amen.

New Year's Eve

O God of our past, present, and future,
　　thank you for the year that is ending.
Thank you for the gift
　　of the year that is beginning.
Thank you for our days and nights,
　　for many memories
　　and for all the ways
　　that you are a part of our lives.
Bless us in this coming year
　　and help us to grow
　　in our love of you
　　and of one another.
Amen.

Parent's Note: Having a clock and/or calendar at hand for this prayer
helps make the intangible reality of time a bit more tangible for everyone.

On a Winter Day

Dear God,
    outside it's cold
    and everything looks nearly dead.
But inside the trees and plants
    new life is beginning to stir.
Even though we have to bundle up
    when we go outside,
    the days of spring aren't too far away.
Thanks for the cold and wet days
    as well as the warm and sunny ones.
Thank you for all your gifts.
Amen.

Valentine's Day

Loving God,
    today we celebrate love.
Because you love us
    we can love one another
    and give one another valentines.
Thank you for love
    and for those who love us.
Thank you especially
    for showing us how to love.
Amen.

Lent

Dear God,
    it's time for Lent,
    to watch the days
    get longer
    and the world
    come to life
    as we wait for Easter.
It's a time to
    think about
    how we can
    love you more.
Help us to remember to pray
    during these forty days,
    and to treat others as Jesus did,
    with love and forgiveness.
Amen.

Parent's Note: Forty days is a long time for children to wait. One way to ease the waiting is to make a lenten picture with forty spaces to color in, one for each day. Your picture can be in the shape of a butterfly, which is a symbol for resurrection, or a tree with many branches, or a path that leads to Easter.

Another activity we enjoy in our home is giving each family member a pretzel, each night of Lent. Tradition has it that the crossed form of a pretzel resembles arms folded in prayer, and thus reminds us that Lent is a time for prayer. (The original name for pretzel was "bracellae," or little arms.)

Palm Sunday

Dear God,
    today we celebrate the day
    the people of Jerusalem
    welcomed Jesus
    with a parade.
They waved palm branches
    like flags and then
    laid them on the ground
    so that Jesus' donkey
    could walk on the palms.
That day, the people of Jerusalem
    knew Jesus was someone special;
    but they forgot in a few days,
    and put him to death
    on the cross.
Please help us never to forget
    how special Jesus is
    in our lives.
Amen.

Parent's Note: This could be a good occasion for a parade at your house, complete with palms from church, pans or other rhythm instruments, and a rousing march song, such as "When the Saints Go Marching In."

Holy Thursday

Dear God,
   tonight we remember the meal
   Jesus shared with his friends
   on the night before he died.
He shared bread and wine with them
   and told them that if they did this, too,
   even after he died he would be with them.
Tonight, our meal may not seem special,
   but every meal is special
   because God celebrates it with us.
Help us to remember
   that you are always with us.
Amen.

Parent's Note: You may want to have grape juice and some flatbread or matzoh (available at most grocery stores) with your evening meal. You may also want to read the biblical account of the Last Supper tonight.

Good Friday

Dear God,
    today is the day we remember
    Jesus' death on the cross.

Some of the people of Jerusalem
    wanted him dead
    and so they arrested him,
    whipped him, and made fun of him.
Many of the people
    who loved him and followed him
    ran away and hid,
    because they were afraid.
After the soldiers made Jesus
    carry his own cross
    they nailed him to it,
    and he hung there until he died.
Later some of his friends came
    and took his body away to bury it.
Please help us to understand
    how much you love us,
    that Jesus would die for us.
Help us, too, to understand
    that you are sad
    when we hurt someone
    to make them feel sad.
When we see a picture of Jesus
    on the cross
    with his arms stretched wide,
    help us remember
    you love us
    that much and more. Amen.

Easter

Loving God,
    this is a time of bunnies and chicks,
    and baskets of colored eggs,
    and new clothes and candy.
But this day is so much more.
It's a time for us to celebrate
    that Jesus is alive.
After he was put to death on the cross,
    he was buried in the tomb.
But when his friends went back to see him
    he wasn't there
    because he had risen from the dead.
Jesus promises us that just as death
    was not the end for him,
    it won't be for us either;
    we'll live with him forever.
Thank you
    for the new life
    around us,
    and especially
    for Jesus.
Amen.

40

On a Spring Day

Dear God,
    the world feels very alive today,
    with birds and flowers
    and many colors.
Thank you for the new life
    we feel and see all around us,
    life that comes from you.
Thank you
    for butterflies and dandelions
    and new leaves and bugs
    and kites and baseball.
Thank you for life.
Amen.

Mother's Day

Dear God,
>   today we celebrate a special person,
>   our mom.
She's a gift of love to us
>   in so many ways.
She's there when we need someone
>   to listen to us.
She cares for us
>   when we're sick or hurt.
She makes our home
>   a warmer place to be.
She helps us learn
>   so many things.
In fact, it's easy to forget
>   all the ways
>   in which she shows
>   her love for us
>   and teaches us about you.
Help her to know
>   how much we love her
>   and how much
>   you love her, too.
We're sure glad you gave her to us.
Amen.

Father's Day

Loving God,
    thanks for our dad.
Thanks for all the wonderful ways
    that he shows us he loves us:
    playing with us,
    taking us places,
    fixing things for us,
    teaching us about life and about you.
Thanks for all the ways he works hard
    to be your love for us.
Please help us to show how much we love him,
    and help him be
    the best dad he can be.
Amen.

Graduation

Dear God,
Hooray! (Name) has just graduated!
She (He) has used the gifts you gave her (him)
   to learn about the world in which we live.
Now she (he) is ready to begin
   a new part of her (his) life.
Please help her (him)
   as she (he) heads in a new direction.
Keep her (him) close to you
   and always growing in love.
   We ask your blessings
      in a special way
         on this day when we celebrate
            a job well done
             and the start of new possibilities.
            Amen.

Last Day of School

Dear God,
    school is out for this year.
We can't wait
    to experience the possibilities
    of summer and vacation.
Thank you for all
    we've learned
    this year.
Thank you for all the
    memories
    and friends
    that have filled
    this year.
Please help us
    not to forget them
    and not to forget
    you, either.
And thank you that school's out!
Amen.

Parent's Note: During the summer look for ways to keep children aware of God in their lives, with activities such as a prayer of thanks for a special day, skits or plays about Bible stories, and reading the lives of the saints.

Going on a Vacation

Dear God,
Thanks for the chance
    to go on this trip together.
Along with the things
    we've packed,
    help us to take
    some wonder
    for the new things
    we will see
    and a lot of
    patience
    with each other.
Please keep us safe
    as we travel.
Watch over our house
    and the friends
    we leave behind.
Help us play, relax,
    and enjoy each other.
And when we come home,
    please help us to see
    in a new way
    what a good place
    our home really is.
Amen.

Fourth of July

Dear God,
Thank you for picnics and families,
    for hotdogs and hamburgers,
    for ice cream and watermelon,
    for fireworks and flags,
    for summer and freedom
    and a good country to live in.
Please bless those
    who don't have all that we do
    and help us to use our freedom
    to make all your people happy.
Amen.

On a Summer Day

Loving God,
    thank you for summer.
Thanks for the sun,
    keeping us warm
    helping things grow.
Thanks for water,
    to drink and to play in,
    in sprinklers and in squirt guns.
Thanks for long days and warm evenings,
    with more time to enjoy
    all you've given us.
Thanks for shorts and swimsuits,
    popsicles and picnics,
    camps and parks,
    lakes and oceans,
    the beautiful world
    you've created.
Help us to enjoy this world
    and take good care of it
    and love you
    in the midst
    of a wonder-filled
    summer.
Amen.

SPECIAL
OCCASION
PRAYERS

Birthday

Dear God,
    today we thank you for (Name).
Thank you for the gift he (she) is to each of us;
    without him (her) we wouldn't be the same.
Thank you for all the ways
    he (she) has brought
    life to all of us
    and shown us your presence.
Please continue to bless him (her)
    as you have for the past _____ years
    and keep him (her) close to you.
Please help him (her) to continue to learn
    more about you
    and to love you more each day.
Amen.

(Now have everyone sing
"Happy Birthday to You,"
perhaps with a second
verse of "May the
good Lord bless you.")

Patron Saint's Day

Loving God,
    today we remember St. (Name),
    the patron saint of (Name).
Thank you for all the
    special people
    who have gone
    before us
    to show us how
    to love you.
Let us see that you
    call each of us
    to love you with
    all our hearts
    and to be a saint, too.
Help (name) to learn more
    about his (her) patron saint
    and to ask that saint's help
    in trying to love you better.
Amen.

Parent's Note: Try to find the feast of your child's patron saint and mark it on the family calendar. A special dessert or meal can help make this a day of note.

Parents' Anniversary

Dear God,
    ___years ago
    our parents
    promised to love each other forever.
Thank you for the ways
    that they show us your love.
Watch over them
    and help them to keep growing
    in love of each other and of you.
Thank you for their love
    which we celebrate today.
  Amen.

New Baby

Dear God,
    you've given our family new life
    through this little baby.
It's amazing to think
    that each of us
    was once that small,
    with tiny fingers and toes.
Help us to care
    for this new life
    you've given us,
    and to fill
    (baby's Name) world
    with love
    and the knowledge
    of you.
Amen.

Parent's Note: Following this prayer, you can ask each family member to bless the baby by making a sign of the cross on his or her forehead.

Baptism

Loving God,
   thank you for giving us
   the gift of Baptism,
   a time to celebrate
   being part of the church.
You give us new life
   and the light of faith;
   let us appreciate this gift
   and all your gifts.
Thank you for those
   who help us learn
   about your love:
   our family, our godparents,
   and our local church.
Thank you for calling us
   to be Christians
Watch over us as we learn
   to better love
   and follow you.
   Amen.

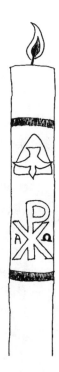

Parent's Note: This prayer may be used either on the day of baptism
or on the anniversary of the child's baptism.

First Communion

Dear God,
    thank you for the opportunity
      (Name) has today
    to share at the table of the Lord.
She (he) has been preparing for this day
    and knows that Jesus is present
    in a special way
    in the bread and wine.
She (he) also knows
    that in receiving Jesus' body and blood
    she (he) is taking her (his) place
    at the family table
    of the community of faith, the church.
Help her (him) to continue to grow in faith,
    and thank you for the chance to celebrate
    a big step in growing closer to you.
Amen.

Confirmation

Loving God,
    thank you for the gift
    of your Spirit
    that you have given (Name)
    in a special way today.
Help him (her) to live
    with kindness peacefulness,
    justice, and wisdom.
Let his (her) faith, hope, and love
    grow stronger every day,
    and let him (her) turn to you
    for guidance and strength.
Let him (her) know
    how much you love him (her).
Help him (her) to share
    your spirit with others
    that he (she) meets.
Amen.

Wedding Day

Dear God,
    today (Name) and (Name) were married
    and promised to love each other
    for the rest of their lives.
We pray that your love will be with them
    to help them keep that promise
    and learn how to love each other unselfishly.
Please keep them in love with each other
    as well as with you.
Let them allow each other
    to become all that they can be
    and to love any children they may have.
Thank you for their love,
    which gives us a glimpse of your love.
Amen.

New House

Dear God,
    thank you for our new house.
It seems strange to have to think
    where things are now
    rather than just to know.
Please help this house to be a place
    where we learn to love each other
    and you better.
Watch over us here.
Help us to make new friends,
    while we stay in touch with old friends.
Bless in a special way
    those families
    that don't have
    a nice place to live in,
    as we do.
Keep them safe
    in your love
    as you keep us here
    in our new house.
Amen.

Parent's Note: Use this prayer after a move, even if the house is just "new" to your family. You may want to go from room to room, saying a short prayer of blessing for each room.

Death in the Family

Loving God,
    we are sad, because (Name) has died.
We know that she (he) is with you
    and that she (he) is very happy now.
We will miss her (him).
We remember all the special ways
    that she (he) was a gift to us:
    the love, happiness, and courage
    that she (he) shared.
Please help us to keep remembering her (him)
    and to hope for the day
    we will be together again
    with her (him) and with you.
Amen.

Parent's Note: This prayer may also be used to remember a child who has died at birth or through miscarriage, omitting the sentence that begins "We remember all...." You may also want to use this prayer on the anniversary of a loved one's death.

Blessing of a Pet

Dear God,
 today we welcome (Name)
 as a part of our family.
We know that (Name)
 depends on us
 to take care of him (her).
Help us to care for him (her)
 and to care for all creatures
 of the world.
Just as we can hold (name)
 and keep him (her) safe,
 so you keep us safe
 and always love us.
Amen.

Death of a Pet

Dear God,
    we loved our pet,
    (Name) very much.
And now (Name)
    has gone back to the earth.
We have many good memories of (Name)
    and the fun we used to have.
(Name) was our friend
    and will always
    be special to us.
We ask you to fill up
    the empty space in our hearts
    and to let something beautiful grow
    from the earth where
    (Name) rests.
Amen.

In a Thunderstorm

Dear God,
     it's rumbling and flashing outside,
     and it feels pretty scary.
Sometimes,
     when the weather is like this,
     it seems like you're
     angry with the world.
Help me to remember
     that you love us
     and want us to be safe...
     then I can enjoy
     the natural fireworks show!
Amen.

Being Sick

Loving God,
    it isn't fun being sick.
I'm tired of lying here in bed
    with nothing much to do.
I know that you love me
    and care about me
    even when I don't think about you.
Please be with me in a special way
    while I'm feeling this bad.
Help me to imagine myself
    climbing up on Jesus' lap
    and getting a hug from him
    as he did for the children
    who came to him when he was teaching.
Please help me to get well soon;
    especially bless those children
    who won't ever get well.
Amen.

Planting a Garden

Dear God,
    we're planting a garden.
The soil is ready,
    and now we can put in the seeds or plants.
The dirt may seem lifeless,
    as do the tiny seeds
    and the water we'll use here;
But everything is full of life
    and full of you.
Thank you for life and for growing.
Please help us understand
    that growing takes patience and waiting.
Help us wait while we are growing,
    as we wait for this garden
    to blossom and grow
    in ways we can hardly imagine now.
Amen.

Finding a Bug
(or Rock, or Flower)

Wow, God.
I just found something very special.
I almost missed it,
 but you had it there, waiting
 as a surprise for me.
Thank you for this discovery,
 and for the eyes to see it.
Help me to keep looking for
 the wonders
 you've made all around us,
   especially the little ones
    that people often miss.
    Amen.

Learning a New Skill

Loving God,
    today I learned how to do something new.
There were days when I thought
I'd never be able to do it,
    but now I can.
With your help, I keep growing in what I can do.
There are lots of things
    I want to learn to do:
Please give me the courage and patience
    to try them.
Let me know
    that you give me
    the ability
    to learn
    new skills.
Thanks
    for helping me
    learn to do
    something new
    today.
Amen.

Parent's Note: Say this prayer in celebration of an accomplishment, such as learning how to whistle, to ride a bike, or how to swim.

For a Friend

Loving God,
    thank you for my friend, (Name).
To know that we like each other
    and want to be friend
    is a special gift.
Thank you for the fun things
    we do together.
Please help me to be a good friend
    and to remember that you
    are always my friend.
Amen.

Parent's Note: This prayer can also be used for a friend who has moved away. Adapt the words by using the past tense. You can also add a sentence about the friend and his (her) family being happy in their new home, while not forgetting their past friends.

After a Fight

Dear God,
    we've had a fight,
    and it didn't feel very good.
It's not fun to feel mad or hurt.
We've mostly forgiven each other,
    but that's the really hard part.
I know you don't like it
    when I fight with people;
You like it a lot better
    when we make up.
Please help us learn
    to work out our differences
    without fighting
    and to forgive and make up
    when we do fight.
Amen.

Winning the Game

Dear God,
    we won!!!
It feels good to know
    that our team
    played well
    and that we beat
    the other team.
Thanks for the happiness
    we feel as a team.
Let the other team
    know that
    just because
    they lost today
    doesn't mean
    they're a bad team,
    or that they won't
    win another time.
Help us to enjoy playing
    whether we win or lose.
Amen.

Losing the Game

Dear God,
　　today we lost the game.
It was hard to lose after we tried our best.
We feel disappointed and sad,
　　but we still enjoyed playing.
Let us know that we're still a good team
　　who can win another day.
Maybe you want us to learn
　　some things by losing,
　　like how much you love us
　　whether we win or lose.
Help us learn what we need to do
　　so that we can play
　　even better another day.
Thank you for our team.
Amen.

New Vehicle
(car, bicycle, riding toys)

Loving God,
     please bless this new (name vehicle).
Please keep those who ride in (on) it
     happy, healthy, and safe.
Let us see the world in a new way
     and know how beautifully you made it.
We ask you to bless all our goings
     and comings back.
Amen.

Parent's Note: Use a lighted candle (carefully!) to make the blessing of
the new vehicle a bit more special.

Losing a Tooth

Dear God,
    I lost a tooth today.
It's another sign that I'm growing up
    and leaving behind the baby me.
Help me to keep growing as you want me to,
    to be kinder and more caring for others
    as I move closer to you.
Thank you for signs like this tooth
    which remind me that I'm changing
    and growing up.
Amen.

Feeling Lonely

Dear God,
　　today I feel lonely.
I don't have any friends
　　that I can play with
　　or anyone I want to be with today.
You've told me that
　　you will always be my friend
　　and that I never
　　need to feel alone.
That makes me feel a bit better.
It's good to remember
　　that you're always with me.
Amen.

Feeling Bored

Dear God,
   today I feel
   bored, bored, bored...
I just don't know
   what to do with myself.
The things I'm usually
   interested in
   don't sound interesting
   or fun today.
Maybe it's because
   I'm just thinking of me.
Could I make
   or do something
   for someone else,
   someone
   who could use a lift, too?
Help me use this energy
   that doesn't know where to go
   to do something nice
   for someone else.
   Amen.

Suggested Resources

Chervin, Ronda de Sola and Conley, Carla. *The Book of Catholic Customs and Traditions: Enhancing Holidays, Special Occasions, and Family Celebrations*. Ann Arbor, MI: Servant Publications, 1994. The title and subtitle of this book say it all.

Chesto, Kathleen. *Family Prayer for Family Times: Traditions, Celebrations, and Rituals*. Mystic, CT: Twenty-Third Publications, 1995. This comprehensive book contains both contemporary and traditional prayers, along with celebrations and rituals for all occasions.

DeGidio, Sandra. *Enriching Faith Through Family Celebrations*. Mystic, CT: Twenty-Third Publications, 1989. A good source-book on ritual in general, with specific rituals for times in the liturgical year.

Finley, Mitch. *Your Family in Focus: Appreciating What You Have, Making It Even Better*. Notre Dame, IN: Ave Maria Press, 1993. A good introduction to seeing daily family life as holy.

Hays, Edward. *Prayers for the Domestic Church: A Handbook for Worship in the Home*. Leavenworth, KS: Forest of Peace Books, 1989. An excellent source of prayers for families with adolescents or adults.

Luebering, Carol. *Your Child's First Communion: A Look at Your Dreams*. Cincinnati, OH: St. Anthony Messenger Press, 1984. This small booklet helps parents understand First Communion in light of the family as the basic religious community.

Meehan, Bridget Mary. *Prayers, Activities, Celebrations (and More) for Catholic Families*. Mystic, CT: Twenty-Third Publications, 1995. Plenty of good ideas will be found here, focusing on how to help family members grow in faith and love.

National Conference of Catholic Bishops. *Following the Way of Love: A Pastoral Message of the U.S. Catholic Bishops to Families*. Washington, D.C.: United States Catholic Conference, 1994. This highly readable document clearly affirms the holiness of families as the domestic church.

Nelson, Gertrud Mueller. *To Dance With God: Family Ritual and Community Celebration*. Mahwah, NJ: Paulist Press, 1986. Drawn primarily from a rich European heritage, this book is a prayerful meditation on the seasons of the church year with many ideas for family ritual.

Roberto, John, et al. *Family Rituals and Celebrations (Catholic Families Series)*. New Rochelle, NY: Don Bosco Press, 1992. A good resource for family prayer with a helpful section on ethnic celebrations.

Travnikar, Rock. *The Blessing Cup: 40 Simple Rites for Family Prayer-Celebrations*. Cincinnati, OH: St. Anthony Messenger Press, 1994. This book uses a special cup as the focus around which family prayer is offered.